Published by Shadowlight Publishing

© 2024

Shadowlight Publishing reserves the rights to all written material within this publication. There will be no duplication without express written permission of Shadowlight Publishing or Elizabeth Waterhouse

978-1-7636-761-8-3

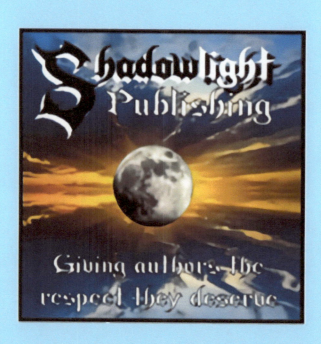

The older I become the more I realise, to be able to share life with the ones you love, it is all that matters. An even bigger bonus is when you dance together creatively. Thank you, Lord R.e Taylor I love you so and am eternally grateful for my dancing partner!

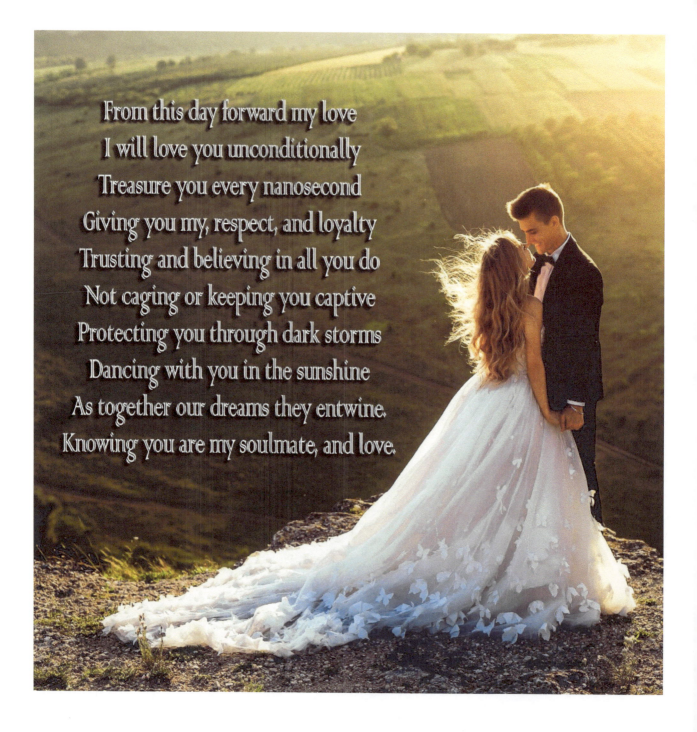

From this day forward my love
I will love you unconditionally
Treasure you every nanosecond
Giving you my, respect, and loyalty
Trusting and believing in all you do
Not caging or keeping you captive
Protecting you through dark storms
Dancing with you in the sunshine
As together our dreams they entwine.
Knowing you are my soulmate, and love.

I will dance with you on a Silvery Moon
We will fly to mountains high
I will love you till my bones they crack
Along with a bloody aching back
I share my life with you and sing you songs
And make love till your seeing stars
One day I may forget your Birthday
And quite often I let the dinner burn
I will drive you nuts, and talk too much
But cherish you till the end of time
My life, my soul mate, my one true love

To give birth to a new baby
Fills your heart to overflowing
You both now are parents
Entrusted with the welfare of a child
A responsibility to last a lifetime
Love this child with all your heart
Provide a shelter from any storm
A haven where they always feel safe
Teach them right from wrong
And to find a world filled with love
And cherish them more than life itself.

We may not have riches supreme
And we may not change the world
But we have each other to love
Our beloved family and friends
And a place to rest our head
And for us that is enough
We give thanks for a life truly blessed.

Dear Father, you have taught me so much
To be the best that I can possibly be
To not always look through rose coloured glasses
To realise that life is never smooth sailing
That we must work for what we want out of life
To recognize those who are sincere and speak the truth
To discard those who flatter and speak with false tongue
To be honest and never lie to others or oneself
Knowing that love, family and friends are riches
That money and success can never buy or compare
Thank you for your wisdom for being such a loving father
You are my strength, and my guide, and I love you so.

To have loving grandparents
Is a blessing for any child
Grandparents love unconditionally
Providing a second shelter of love
Through sunny and stormy days
Offering advice, wisely worth taking
Holidays never the same without them
Grandparents are to be appreciated
And to be treasured and loved always

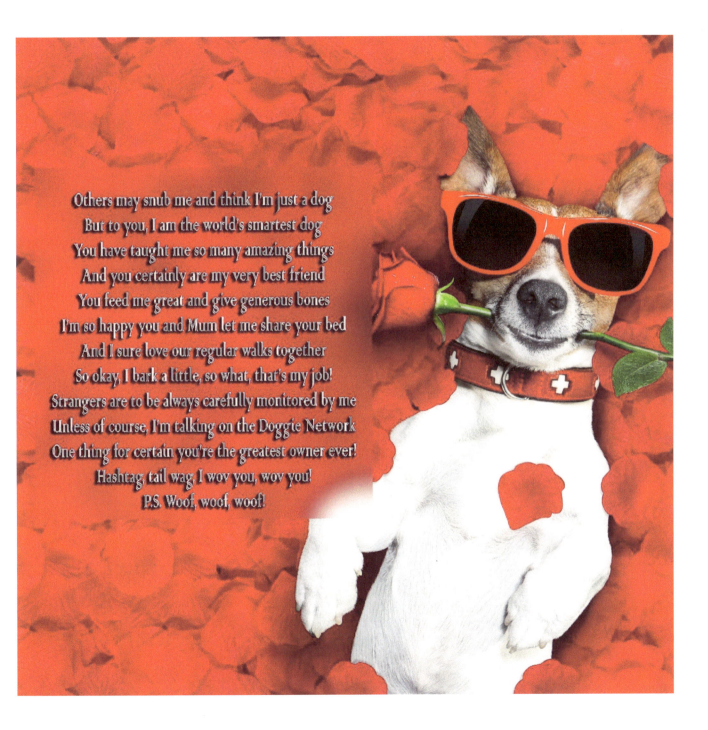

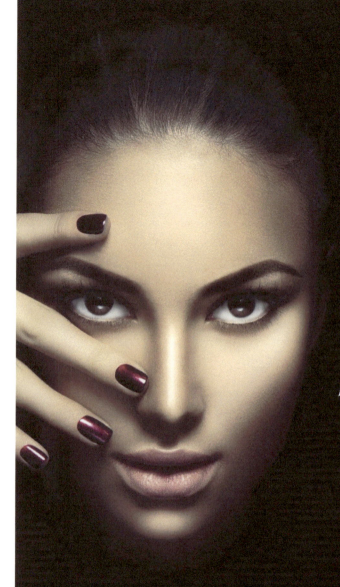

She gazed at him with haunting eyes

To him she was utterly perfect

As love embraced him for the first time

His young heart was lost for words

Totally smitten all he desired was her.

Always confide in the one you love
Do not hide and keep secrets
Open your heart and tell it as it is
Then you will know if you are truly loved

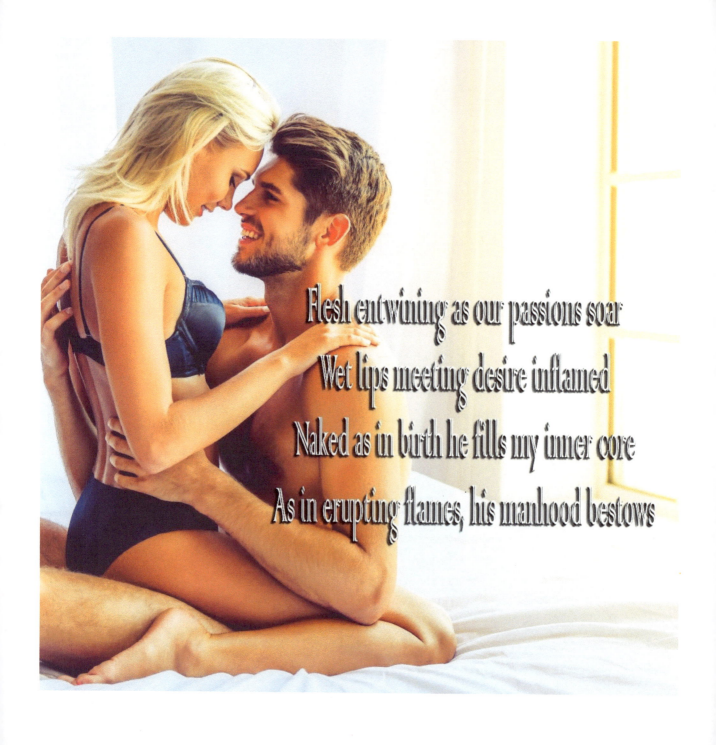

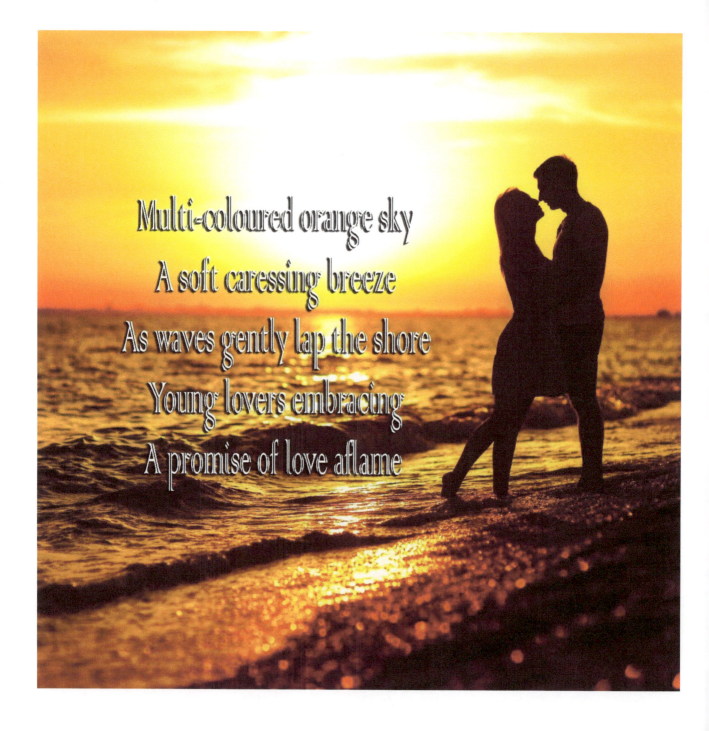

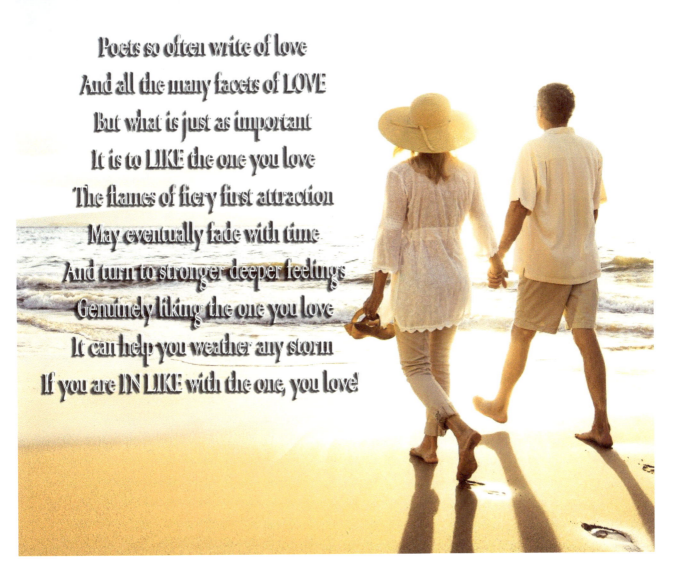

Poets so often write of love
And all the many facets of LOVE
But what is just as important
It is to LIKE the one you love
The flames of fiery first attraction
May eventually fade with time
And turn to stronger deeper feelings
Genuinely liking the one you love
It can help you weather any storm
If you are IN LIKE with the one, you love!

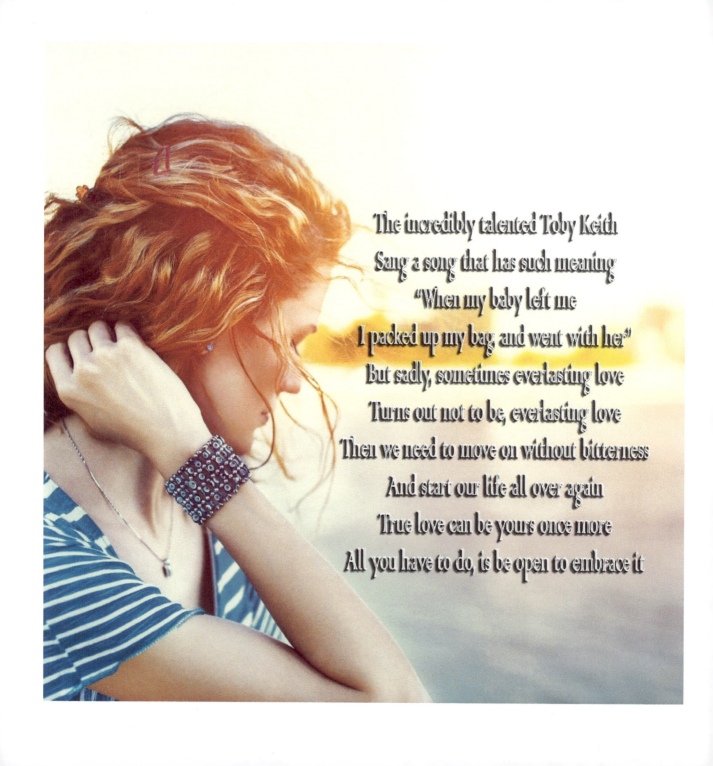

The incredibly talented Toby Keith
Sang a song that has such meaning
"When my baby left me
I packed up my bag and went with her"
But sadly, sometimes everlasting love
Turns out not to be, everlasting love
Then we need to move on without bitterness
And start our life all over again
True love can be yours once more
All you have to do, is be open to embrace it

Someone once stated love is free
Oh no, oh no, my friend, love is not free
In fact, love is the total opposite of free
It takes and binds your very being
It requires utter truth in all its forms
Utter devotion in times of great turmoil
Loyalty when the rest of the world is against
Undying belief, tolerance and total empathy
Hope, humour, and Herculean strength
It demands the giving of your inner core
Oh no, oh no, my friend love is not free
But in its gaining, it is the ultimate treasure

Love me with words, sweet tender words
Covet me, covet me as men covet power
Hold me, caress me with awesome wonder
Want me with a burning, flaming need
With uncontrollable longing and desire
Tender my garden so the roses bloom
Make of me your soulmate, your everything
And my heart will soar to the heavens above.

Milton Keynes UK
Ingram Content Group UK Ltd.
UKHW050229021224
451757UK00002B/4